MIND YOUR LANGUAGE!

ENGLISH FOR NANNIES AND AU PAIRS

JENNIFER BRUMMER

WAYZGOOSE PRESS

CONTENTS

CHAPTER 4: "WHAT DO YOU WANT FOR DINNER?"

CHAPTER 5: "OW, I HURT MYSELF!"

LETTER FROM THE AUTHOR

Dear Readers,

Shaping children's lives is one of the most important jobs in the world and you have chosen to do it. You must be a very special person!

When English is not your first language, working with English speaking children and families might be challenging. This book will help you practice English language skills that you will use many times throughout your job: communicating with parents, discipline and sibling rivalry, homework help, food, and health and safety.

This is a self-study book. That means you can learn everything by yourself, and you don't need a teacher. You can move through each chapter as fast or as slow as you'd like. You can repeat anything, and you can focus on what you feel you need the most. However, it is recommended that you start at Chapter 1 and finish at Chapter 5, because each chapter becomes increasingly more difficult.

I would like to thank my husband Richard Brummer for being so supportive of all of my dreams and goals. My dear friend and colleague Shaza Mahmood contributed towards many of the reading exercises in this book. Thank you for all your guidance and help, Shaza. Of course, a massive thank you to our amazing editor and publisher, Maggie Sokolik and Dorothy Zemach.

I am excited for you because I know that this book will help you be confident and successful in your job. When you complete this book, you will feel very satisfied.

Best of luck to you!

Warmest Regards,

Jennifer Brummer, Author

THE STRUCTURE OF THE BOOK

This book is organized in chapters and sections. This chart shows what you will find in each part.

Chapter	Conversation Skill	Language Point	Reading
Chapter 1 *"So, what did you do all day?"*	How to explain your day to the parents	Simple and Continuous Past, WH- questions	*Communicating with Children and Parents*
Chapter 2 *"He started it!"*	How to handle discipline and sibling rivalry	Connecting words expressing cause and effect	*Problems and Solutions*
Chapter 3 *"What do you have for homework today?"*	How to help children with their homework	Conditionals with 'if' clauses	*Stargazing Journal*
Chapter 4 *"What do you want for dinner?"*	How to talk about food	Suggestions	*Dealing with Fussy Eaters*
Chapter 5 *"Health and Safety"*	How to use basic medical English	Modals and Adverbs	*Notice Board*

GRAMMAR/VOCABULARY EXPLANATIONS

N = noun; a person, place or thing. I am a *nanny*. "Nanny" is a noun.

V = verb; an action word. Jack *likes* oatmeal. "Like" is a verb.

Adj. = adjective; a word used to describe a noun. She is an *adorable* child. "Adorable" is an adjective.

Adv. = adverb; a word used to describe a verb or an adjective. Let's speak *quietly* when we are inside the library. "Quietly" is an adverb.

Phrase = a group of words that are used together. We *need to make a move,* so please get your shoes on. "Make a move" is a phrase.

Article = a, the, or an. Look at *the* flower. "The" is an article.

NOTE: The articles of nouns are included in the vocabulary tables in this book, but they might not be needed in the fill-in-the-blank activities. When you are doing the fill-in-the-blank activities, you must decide if you will need an article or not. For verbs, you may need to use a 'to' with the infinitive, or you may not. Again, fill in the blanks with the correct forms.

CHAPTER 1: "WHAT DID YOU DO ALL DAY?"

HOW TO EXPLAIN YOUR DAY TO THE PARENTS

When parents ask how the day went with their children, how do you answer it? Sometimes, it can be difficult to have this conversation in English.

The activities in Chapter 1 will help you build the confidence to *understand* and *explain* activities to the children at your job.

CONVERSATION

Read the conversation between a father and a nanny, Marie.

Father: How was your day?

Marie: It was great! We had a lot of fun today.

Father: Really? That's wonderful. So, what did you do all day?

Marie: Well, first, the kids had breakfast.

Father: What did they eat?

Marie: Benjamin ate half a bagel with some strawberries on the side, and Hannah ate some oatmeal with her milk.

Father: Okay, that sounds good. What happened after breakfast?

Marie: I walked them to the park, in the double stroller.

Father: Did you remember the sunscreen and the hats?

Marie: Yes.

Father: Great. Thank you. How long were you playing at the park?

Marie: We were there for almost two hours, I think. Benjamin was running around with his friend who was also there.

Father: That's nice. Which friend was spending time there?

Marie: Michael. I was talking with his parents. They are really nice.

Father: Yes, they are. So, what did they eat for lunch?

Marie: Benjamin wanted some macaroni and cheese, and I gave Hannah mashed sweet potatoes.

Father: Okay, how long were they napping?

Marie: Benjamin slept for an hour and a half, and Hannah only napped for about twenty minutes. Hannah woke Benjamin up when she started to cry.

Father: That certainly sounds like my Hannah. She is always waking us up!

Listen to Chapter 1 Conversation 1:
mindyourlanguage.us/audio-files/

Pause after you hear Marie and repeat her responses two to three times, until it feels natural. Do not read when you repeat. Look in a mirror instead.

DID YOU UNDERSTAND?

1. Who ate a bagel?
2. Who ate oatmeal?
3. How did they get to the park?

    A) She pulled them in the wagon.

    B) They rode bikes.

    C) She pushed them in the double stroller.

4. What did Benjamin do at the park?

    A) He went on the swings and the slide.

    B) He ran around with Michael.

    C) He played in the sandbox.

5. What did Hannah have for lunch?
6. Why did Benjamin wake up?

LANGUAGE POINT: SIMPLE PAST & CONTINUOUS VERBS

WH- Questions

When parents ask questions about your day with their children, they will sometimes ask in simple past tense, and other times, they will ask in continuous past (verbs with *-ing*).

Tip: Try to copy the way they speak.

If they ask you a question in *simple past* form, you can answer in *simple past* form. If they ask you a question in *continuous past* form, you can answer in *continuous past* form.

The main difference between the two forms is this: Simple past tense is an action in the past. Continuous Past also takes place in the past, but for a longer time.

Let's take a closer look:

What a parent asks	How you answer
Simple Past WH- question	**Simple Past answer**
Where | did | the kids | go this morning? *Wh- | did | subject | verb…*	**They | went | to the park.** *Subject | past verb …|*
Continuous Past WH- question	**Continuous Past answer**
What | were | they | doing | at 12: 00? *Wh- | was/were | subject | verb +- ing…*	**They | were | eating | lunch.** *Subject | was/were | verb + ing…*

Language Point: Activity 1

Answer the questions in full sentences. The first one is done as an example.

1. Why did the kids fight? (*toy* | *break*) **<u>The kids fought because the toy broke.</u>**
2. What did she eat for dinner? (*spaghetti and meatballs*)
3. Why was the baby crying? (*tired*)

4. Who was Jenny talking to on the phone? (*her best friend*)
5. How long were they watching TV? (30 *minutes*)
6. When did they fall asleep? (8:00)
7. How long was he working on his math homework? (30 *minutes*)
8. What did they have for snack? (*watermelon*)

Language Point: Activity 2

Create your own sentences using the words.

Example Question: she + share + favorite toy (past simple)

Possible Answer: *"She shared her favorite toy with her friend. I am so proud of her."*

1. kids + play + basketball (continuous past)
2. she + eat + sandwich (simple past)
3. they + do + homework (simple past)
4. she + nap + two hours (continuous past)

VOCABULARY

Look at these words. Which ones do you already know?

	I can use this word when I speak.	I know what this word means, but I don't use it.	I don't know this word.
a variety			
a routine			
sunscreen			
an indication			
expected			
detailed			
confidence			
spoiled			
a highlight			
a virus			

If you don't know some of these words, look them up in the glossary at the end of this chapter. Be sure you can use them when you speak.

Vocabulary Activity

Which words from the table belong in the blanks? The first one is done as an example.

1. I really like the <u>*variety*</u> in my job. Every day, there is something different to do and experience.
2. It is very important to tell parents ___________ descriptions of what you do with their children.
3. Don't forget to put on ___________ to protect your skin.
4. I think he had a 24-hour ___________. He feels much better today.
5. The ___________ of my day was when she said, "I love you so much!"
6. I want the kids to have ___________, so I praise them often.
7. Her letter of recommendation gave me a good ___________ of how she felt about the work I did for her family.
8. The children know that after I read them a story, they take a nap. It is part of their daily ___________.
9. In my house, good behavior is not rewarded. It is ___________.
10. I did not give them milk today because it was past the expiration date and ___________.

More Practice

Part 1: Read the questions that were seen in the conversation in the beginning of this chapter. How would you answer them in your own words? Write your answers down and practice saying them until it feels natural. (*Note: Do not listen to the audio files yet. This will happen in Part 2.*)

Example:

Father: *How was your day?*

Possible idea:

You: *It was great, thanks. We had so much fun today.*

1. **Father**: How was your day? (*Chapter 1, Ideas 1-1*)

You:

2. **Father**: What did they eat? (*Chapter 1, Ideas 1-2*)

You:

3. **Father**: What happened after breakfast? (*Chapter 1, Ideas 1-3*)

You:

4. **Father**: Did you remember the sunscreen and the hats? (*Chapter 1, Ideas 1-4*)

You:

5. **Father**: How long were you playing at the park? (*Chapter 1, Ideas 1-5*)

You:

6. **Father**: So, what did they eat for lunch? (*Chapter 1, Ideas 1-6*)

You:

7. **Father**: Okay, how long did they nap? (*Chapter 1, Ideas 1-7*)

You:

Part 2: Go to mindyourlanguage.us/audio-files/ and listen to each question. Pause the audio after the question is asked, and answer it in your own words. Then, restart the audio to hear more ways you could answer the father. Repeat these example answers until it feels natural to you.

PRONUNCIATION

Activity 1

Read the words and phrases aloud. Then listen to them and repeat.

Go to mindyourlanguage.us/audio-files/

Chapter 1 > Pronunciation > Activity 1 > Pronunciation 1

slept | napped | woke up
walked | sunscreen | mashed potato

Activity 2

Listen to the sentences and repeat them aloud. Try practicing the sentences in different ways so that you can use them naturally and confidently in your job.

Go to mindyourlanguage.us/audio-files/

Chapter 1 > Pronunciation > Activity 2

1. She slept for an hour and a half.

2. She napped for only forty minutes, then she woke up crying.
3. She woke up after a nice two-hour nap.
4. She didn't nap for very long. She woke up a little bit cranky.
5. I walked the kids to the park in the double stroller.
6. We walked together to the park after they napped.
7. I put sunscreen on them a half-hour before we left for the park.
8. I reapplied the sunscreen after we had been outside for two hours.
9. She really wanted mashed potatoes with lunch.
10. I gave her a little bit of a mashed sweet potato after she drank her milk.

READING

Communicating with Children and Parents

Read the tips about communicating with children and parents. Do you agree with them?

Tip 1

Having routines will make your days with the children go smoothly. For example, perhaps every day after breakfast, you might try to take the children for a short walk outside. If this is expected, they will know that once they are finished eating, they should help you clear the table and get them ready to go outside. This might include putting on a jacket or some sunscreen, depending on the weather.

Tip 2

Some questions parents might ask you are: "Did he eat all of his lunch?" "How long did he nap?" and "Did she finish her homework?" When you respond, be sure to give detailed stories and not just the highlights of the day. Parents love to hear details of their children's days. It gives them confidence that their child is happy, healthy, and loved by you.

Tip 3

Be sure to call or text the parent if there is a serious issue with their child. For example, if the child throws up after he eats his lunch, it may be an indication that he has virus or that he had eaten something spoiled. The parent must know this information immediately, not a few hours later.

Tip 4

Children enjoy a variety of different activities. Ask your child about his or her favorite things to do. Look online to find some fun activities that he or she might enjoy as well. Some ideas of things you could do with the child at home might be:

- Do an arts and crafts project together
- Play a board game together
- Build something out of wooden blocks
- Dress up in funny costumes and put on a show
- Read a book together

Activity 1

Answer the questions below, based on the reading. Choose true, false, or not given.

1. Taking children for regular walks is good for their development.

   A) True

   B) False

   C) Not given

2. Tip 2 reveals the importance of keeping parents up to date.

A) True

B) False

C) Not given

3. If a child throws up, he or she might have a virus.

A) True

B) False

C) Not given

4. Parents prefer nannies to write down everything their children have done during the day.

A) True

B) False

C) Not given

5. Parents tend to ask how their child's day went.

A) True

B) False

C) Not given

Activity 2

Choose the correct answer.

1. What is an activity that is NOT suggested in the article?

A) Playing dress-up

B) Building things

C) Cooking together

2. According to the article, if the child is having a serious problem, what should the nanny do?

A) Call up a good friend and ask for advice

B) Tell the parents when they get home

C) Let the parents know immediately

3. What can nannies and au pairs do to make the day smoother?

A) Give the child whatever he or she wants

B) Have routines in place so the child knows what to expect

C) Do arts and crafts every day

4. What is suggested to help parents feel confident?

A) Answering all their questions quickly

B) Telling many details about their children's day

C) Saying only good things about their child

5. How does the article suggest finding ways to come up with new activities?

A) Ask the parents

B) Ask the teachers

C) Browse the internet

Answers are found at the end of the chapter.

QUESTIONS FOR THOUGHT

Write the answers to the following questions in a journal. Read through your answers at least once a week before you go to work.

1. Do you think the nanny did a good job answering the mother's questions in the sample conversation? Did she respond with enough details?
2. Pay attention to the number of times you hear someone at your job use either the simple or continuous past tense. Do you find these words used often? Which other types of language do you find commonly used?
3. Choose one or two new words that you just learned in the vocabulary section of this chapter and use them in conversation this week.
4. Record yourself repeating the sentences in the pronunciation section of this chapter. Listen to your recording. Do you think you sound confident and clear? What could you improve?
5. Rate the tips in the "Communicating with Children and Parents" reading passage from most important to least important. What other tips would you add for someone who is about to be a nanny for the first time?

GLOSSARY

- **confidence**

(N) When someone believes in and feels good about himself or herself

Example: *She walked right up to him and introduced herself. She has a lot of* ***confidence****.*

- **cranky**

(Adj.) Irritable; grouchy

Example: *He skipped his nap today so he is extra* ***cranky*** *right now.*

- **detailed**

(Adj.) Having a full description

Example: *Be sure to give her mother a* ***detailed*** *description of what you did today with her. Don't leave anything out.*

- **development**

(N) The process of learning and growing

Example: *Playing imaginative games is so good for the toddler's* ***development****.*

- **discipline**

(N) The process of training children to follow rules and have good behavior

Example: *The mother believed in strict rules and* ***discipline*** *for her child.*

- **a double stroller**

(N) A buggy or push-chair on wheels with two seats

Example: *The twins looked so cute being pushed by their father in their* ***double stroller.***

- **to encourage**

(V) To support and give confidence to someone

Example: *He was scared to go down the slide, but after I* ***encouraged*** *him, he did it!*

- **expected**

(Adj.) Believed to happen

Example: *The clouds were very gray. The rain was* ***expected.***

- **a highlight**

(N) The best part of something

Example: *The **highlight** of my job is getting hugs from my kids.*

- **an indication**

(N) Evidence; a sign

Example: *She didn't say hello to me today. I think this as **an indication** that something was wrong.*

- **macaroni and cheese**

(N) A common food for toddlers made of noodles and cheese sauce

Example: *All he ever wants to eat is **macaroni and cheese**.*

- **oatmeal**

(N) A breakfast food made from ground oats

Example: *She loves to put a little cinnamon on her **oatmeal**.*

- **on the side**

(Phrase) In addition to the main thing or idea

Example: *I will have a hamburger, with some French fries **on the side**.*

- **popular**

(Adj.) Liked by a lot of people

Example: *My son loves that **popular** television show about the boy who solves mysteries.*

- **to prompt**

(V) Brought about by an action or situation

Example: *The sticker chart* ***prompted*** *positive behavior in the child.*

- **to reapply**

(V) To put something on again

Example: *I* ***reapply*** *sunscreen on my children after they have been in the sun for an hour.*

- **a routine**

(N) A regular schedule

Example: *My young children enjoy their evening* ***routine****. They drink milk, brush their teeth, read a story, and sing a song every night before bedtime.*

- **a sandbox**

(N) A box in a playground filled with sand and sand toys, such as shovels and buckets

Example: *His shoes were filled with sand after playing in the* ***sandbox****.*

- **slept**

(V) **Past tense of sleep**

Example: *He* ***slept*** *for ten hours last night.*

- **spoiled**

(Adj.) Gone bad (because of lack of refrigeration or not being eaten or drunk before expiration date)

Example: *The milk smells bad. It's definitely **spoiled**. Don't drink it!*

- **sunscreen**

(N) A lotion that protects skin from the sun

Example: *I got a horrible sunburn because I forgot to apply **sunscreen**.*

- **a variety**

(N) A number of different types of things

Example: *There is a **variety** of children's TV shows on nowadays. When I was young, there were only three or four.*

- **a virus**

(V) A sickness, such as a cold or flu

Example: *The child I watch has a **virus**, so his mom is staying home from work to look after him today.*

- **a wagon**

(N) A toy vehicle that children can sit in (and be pulled around) or that they can fill with toys.

Example: *The kids love the **wagon** I bought them. They pull each other around in it.*

CHAPTER 1 ANSWERS

Did You Understand?

1. Benjamin had a bagel.
2. Hannah had oatmeal.
3. C) He pushed them in the double stroller.
4. B) He ran around with Michael.
5. Hannah had mashed sweet potatoes for lunch.
6. He woke up because Hannah started crying.

Language Point: Activity 1 Possible Answers

1. The kids fought because the toy broke.
2. She ate spaghetti and meatballs for dinner.
3. He was crying because he was tired.
4. She was talking to her best friend on the phone.
5. They were watching TV for a half hour.
6. They fell asleep at 8.
7. He was working on his homework for 30 minutes.
8. They had watermelon for their snack.

Language Point: Activity 2 Possible Answers

1. kids + play + basketball (continuous past)

The kids were playing basketball all afternoon.

2. she + eat + sandwich (simple past)

She ate a peanut butter sandwich for lunch.

3. they + do + homework (simple past)

They did all their homework.

4. she + nap + two hours (continuous past)

She was napping for two hours.

Vocabulary Activity

1. variety
2. detailed
3. sunscreen
4. virus
5. highlight
6. confidence
7. indication
8. routine
9. expected
10. spoiled

Ideas for More Practice

Go to mindyourlanguage.us/audio-files/

Chapter 1 > More Practice

1 *Ideas 1-1*

Father: *How was your day?*

You: It was wonderful. The kids and I had so much fun together.

You: It was really nice, thanks. We had fun!

You: It was a lot of fun. We really enjoyed the day together.

2 *Ideas 1-2*

Father: *What did they eat?*

You: I gave Benjamin half a bagel with some strawberries, and Hannah had her milk with oatmeal.

You: Benjamin enjoyed his bagel but only had half of it. He also had some strawberries. Hannah ate her oatmeal and drank her milk.

You: Benjamin had half a bagel with a few strawberries on the side. Hannah drank milk and ate some oatmeal.

3 *Ideas 1-3*

Father: *What happened after breakfast?*

You: We took a walk to the park. I pushed them in the double stroller.

You: We went to the park. I brought the double stroller so they could both sit in case Benjamin got tired while we walked there.

You: I pushed them in the double stroller down to the park.

4 *Ideas 1-4*

Father: *Did you remember the sunscreen and the hats?*

You: Yes, I brought the baby sunscreen for Hannah and the SPF 50 for Benjamin.

You: Yes I did. I made sure to apply it before we left. They wore their hats, too.

You: Yes. We used both since it was so sunny this morning.

5 Ideas 1-5

Father: *How long were you playing at the park?*

You: Nearly two hours. Benjamin was enjoying his time running around with Michael.

You: Just about two hours. The time really flew while Benjamin was running around with his buddy Michael.

You: Almost two hours. Benjamin had so much fun with Michael.

6 Ideas 1-6

Father: *So, what did they eat for lunch?*

You: Benjamin had his macaroni and cheese, and I mashed up a sweet potato for Hannah.

You: I gave macaroni and cheese to Benjamin, and Hannah had a little bit of a sweet potato.

You: Benjamin requested some macaroni and cheese. I gave Hannah a mashed sweet potato.

7 Ideas 1-7

Father: *Okay, how long did they nap?*

You: Benjamin had a nice hour and a half nap. Unfortunately, he woke up when Hannah started crying after only 20 minutes.

You: Benjamin slept for 90 minutes. Hannah, on the other hand, only had a short nap for 20 minutes. Then she woke up Benjamin.

You: Benjamin had a nice rest. He slept for an hour and a half. Hannah only had a little cat-nap which lasted about 20 minutes. When she started crying, Benjamin woke up.

Reading

Part 1:

1. C
2. A
3. A
4. C
5. A

Part 2:

1. C
2. C
3. B
4. B
5. C

CHAPTER 2: "HE STARTED IT!"

HOW TO HANDLE DISCIPLINE AND SIBLING RIVALRY

When children fight with each other or don't listen to you, how do you handle it?

This is a very difficult topic, even for native English speakers!

The activities in Chapter 2 will give you ways to handle behavior issues in English so that you can *communicate clearly with the children* that you are disciplining.

Conversation

Read the conversation between Jonah, Alex, and their au pair, Mario. Remember to stop the audio playback when you're listening to understand the conversation more clearly.

Jonah: I'm tired.

Alex: Stop complaining! You're so annoying!

Mario: Now, boys, please be nice to each other.

Jonah: He started it!

Alex: No I didn't, you did. Give me that baseball. [*takes the baseball from Jonah*]

Jonah: Give it back!

Mario: Alex, give Jonah back his baseball. You can't have it because it belongs to him.

Alex: Actually, the baseball was mine first, so I can take it back whenever I want.

Mario: I do not appreciate the way you are talking right now. It is very rude. Look at your little brother's face... he is sad. He wants his baseball back. I want to tell your mom you had a good day today...

Alex: I don't care if you give my mom a bad report.

Jonah: Give me my baseball! Now!

Mario: Jonah, we do not behave like this. Alex, please give me the ball now and we'll all take five minutes to cool off. Then we can figure out a solution together.

[5 minutes later]

Mario: Okay, guys. Come sit down. Let's talk about this in a different way. Alex, if you want to ask Jonah to play with his baseball, is there a nicer way to say it?

Alex: I guess.

Mario: Okay... go on.

Alex: Jonah... can I please use your baseball?

Jonah: I'm using it now.

Mario: Jonah, since Alex has asked you in a nice way, the nice thing to do would be to share, right? And wouldn't it be more fun to play with the ball together?

Jonah: Fine. Alex, don't take things from me anymore, okay?

Mario: Alex, if you ask in a respectful way, Jonah is going to be more likely to share his things with you.

Alex: Okay. Fine. Hey Jonah, let's go throw the ball together outside.

Jonah: Sure.

Listen to Chapter 2 Conversation 2. Go to:

mindyourlanguage.us/audio-files/

Pause after you hear Mario and repeat his responses 2-3 times, until it feels natural. Try not to read from the textbook when you repeat. Look in a mirror instead.

DID YOU UNDERSTAND?

1. What did Alex take from Jonah?

2. What does Alex mean when he says *bad report?*

   A) Mario will give the baseball to their mother.

   B) Mario will punish the children.

   C) Mario will tell the boys' mother that they were misbehaving today.

3. What did Mario tell the boys to do for five minutes?

4. After five minutes, the boys:

A) continued to argue a lot.

B) were a little bit stubborn, but soon made peace.

C) were happy right away.

5. Where did they decide to throw the ball?

LANGUAGE POINT: GIVING REASONS

Using words such as ***because***, ***since***, ***now that***, and ***as long as*** will help you give reasons, consequences of behavior, and causes/effects.

Children also use this grammar to explain the reasons behind their actions.

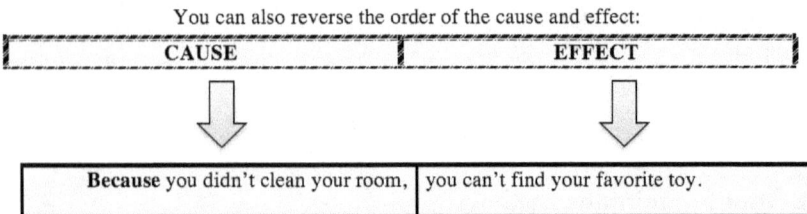

EFFECT	CAUSE
You can't find your favorite toy	**because** you didn't clean your room.

*(**Because** answers the question "why?")*

EFFECT	CAUSE
I was playing my piano	**since** Jessie was using my computer.
Go ahead and have your dessert	**now that** you've eaten your veggies.

*(**Now that** / **since** emphasizes the cause and its effect)*

EFFECT	CAUSE
You can play with Billy's toys	**as long as** he doesn't mind sharing.

*(**As long as** means "only if")*

You can also reverse the order of the cause and effect:

CAUSE	EFFECT
Because you didn't clean your room,	you can't find your favorite toy.

Language Point Activity 1

Match the beginnings of the sentences to their correct endings.

Example: *As long as you continue being disrespectful, you won't get what you want.* **(C)**

1) As long as you continue being disrespectful,	**A)** he is much happier. See how he is smiling now?
2) Please stop! She is crying	**B)** since you did your job today.
3) Now that you have stopped arguing with your brother,	**C)** you won't get what you want.
4) Let's put a sticker on your responsibility chart	**D)** we can go again tomorrow.
5) Remember to clean up your toys while you are playing	**E)** because she wants to be left alone.
6) Do you see how she stopped crying	**F)** you need to use the money from your allowance to buy her a new one.
7) As long as you are both making safe choices at the park,	**G)** because you love playing in a tidy space.
8) Now that you broke her favorite toy,	**H)** now that you are using kind words?

Language Point Activity 2

Create your own sentences using the words below.

Example Question: upset + since + hat

Possible Answer: *"Your sister is upset since you took her hat."*

1. sad + because + toy
2. tired + since + nap
3. now that + friend + share
4. as long as + finished + crayon

VOCABULARY

Look at these words. Which ones do you already know?

	I can use this word when I speak.	I know what this word means, but I don't use it.	I don't know this word.
a tantrum			
a break			
to escalate			
to grab			
to yell			
a concept			
to facilitate			
to encourage			
to solve			
a consequence			

If you don't know some of these words, look them up in the glossary at the end of this chapter. Be sure you can use them when you speak.

VOCABULARY ACTIVITY

Which words from the table belong in the blanks? The first one is done as an example.

1. The nanny will *facilitate* the play time.
2. The problem will ___________ if it is not addressed.
3. The young child just ___________ the cookie from the cookie jar and ran off!
4. He was overwhelmed with big feelings so he threw a ___________.
5. She will go outside once she ___________ her puzzle. (*Hint: add –s*)
6. Children need to learn that there are ___________ to their actions. (Hint: add -s)
7. I ___________ him to taste a new food, but he didn't want to. (*Hint: add -d*)
8. He was ___________ loudly for help! (*Hint: add -ing*)
9. I think you need a five minute ___________ to cool off.

10. The student failed the test because he did not understand the math ___________.

MORE PRACTICE

Part 1: Read the questions that were seen in the conversation in the beginning of this chapter. How would you answer them in your own words? Write your answers down and practice saying them until it feels natural. (*Note: Do not listen to the audio files yet. This will happen in Part 2.*)

Example: *Child: I'm tired.*

Possible idea—*You: I'm sure you are. Would you like to take a short nap?*

1. **Child**: I'm tired. (*Chapter 2, Ideas 2-1*)

You:

2. **Child**: He started it! (*Chapter 2, Ideas 2-2*)

You:

3. **Child**: He took my baseball! (*Chapter 2, Ideas 2-3*)

You:

4. **Child**: I can take the baseball whenever I want to, since it was mine first. (*Chapter 2, Ideas 2-4*)

You:

5. Child: I don't care what you say to my mom. (*Chapter 2, Ideas 2-5*)

You:

6. **Child**: Give me my baseball! Now! (*Chapter 2, Ideas 2-6*)

You:

Part 2: Go to mindyourlanguage.us/audio-files/ and listen to each question. Pause the audio after the question is asked, and answer it in your own words. Then, restart the audio to hear more ways you could respond to the child. Repeat these example answers until it feels natural to you.

PRONUNCIATION

Activity 1

Read the words and phrases aloud. Then listen to them and repeat.

Go to mindyourlanguage.us/audio-files/

Chapter 2 > Pronunciation > Activity 1 > Pronunciation 2

bad report | good report | nicer way
ask him | respectful way | share

Activity 2

Listen to the sentences and repeat them aloud. Try practicing the sentences in different ways so that you can use them naturally and confidently in your job.

Go to mindyourlanguage.us/audio-files/

Chapter 2 > Pronunciation > Activity 2

1. We never want to give your mom a bad report.

2. I would like to give your dad a good report of how you made so many good choices today.
3. Please make a good choice so that I can give your mother a good report later.
4. If you want to ask Jonah to play with his baseball, is there a nicer way to say it?
5. Could you try asking him that in a nicer way?
6. Is there a better way to ask him that?
7. If you ask in a respectful way, he is going to be more likely to share his things with you.
8. If you want him to share with you, you need to speak respectfully.
9. When you are respectful, your friends will respond better to you.
10. Please be respectful.

READING

Problems and Advice

Activity 1

Read the problems in the first list and match them with the best advice from the list below.

Example: *Problem 1 matches best with Advice C.*

Problem 1

Alexis wants to use the toy that her big brother is using, so she grabs it out of his hands. He gets frustrated and takes it back from her. The argument escalates when she throws a tantrum and hits him in the face.

Problem 2

Emma does not want to eat any fruits or vegetables. You encourage her to try a vegetable, but she only wants to eat chicken nuggets and bread.

Problem 3

Brody jumps on the couch every day, even though his parents do not allow that. When you ask him to stop, he starts laughing and does it even more.

Problem 4

Tyrone does not want to do his math homework after school. He says that it is boring and there is no point to doing it.

Problem 5

Elena keeps getting extremely frustrated because her baby sister ruins every project she begins.

Advice A

Since this topic might not be so fun for him, you could make it fun! For every question he solves, he can run outside and kick a soccer ball before answering the next question. He might be happier with short breaks in between answering questions.

Advice B

Facilitate her activities at a table, out of reach from the baby. As long as her work is protected and safe, she will feel relaxed and confident.

Advice C

First, address the hitting because it is the most serious issue. Instead of yelling at her, have her practice using "gentle hands." Once you have discussed the right way to use her hands, you can start talking about the concept of sharing with the children.

Advice D

Do not push the child to eat what they do not wish to eat because it will only make things worse. However, continue to put a small amount of new food on her plate. Sometimes playing a game with the food can help. For example, if you pretend the broccoli is a tree and the child is a dinosaur, they might have fun and try the broccoli.

Advice E

Now that you have asked him to stop, remind him about a time that he got hurt. Getting hurt is a consequence of not making safe choices. Continue to stop him whenever it happens, and direct him to a safe activity.

Activity 2

Answer the questions below, based on the reading.

1. What is suggested for children who are picky eaters?

A) Bribe them with desserts.

B) Try to make eating new foods fun.

C) Do not let them leave the table until they eat all of it.

2. What causes Elena to be frustrated?

A) Her younger sister threw a tantrum and hit her in the face.

B) Her younger sister keeps messing up her projects.

C) Her younger sister doesn't want to do her math homework.

3. What is the most serious issue to address with Alexis and her brother?

A) Sharing

B) Tantrums

C) Hitting

4. What is Brody's usual reaction to being told to stop jumping on the couch?

A) To stop

B) To laugh

C) To cry

5. What are Emma's favorite foods to eat?

A) Broccoli and bread

B) Chicken nuggets and bread

C) Chicken nuggets and broccoli

6. Why doesn't Tyrone want to do his math homework?

A) He thinks it's boring

B) He thinks it's too hard

C) He thinks it's exciting

7. What is a suggested game for eating broccoli?

A) Pretending it is a tree

B) Pretending it is chocolate

C) Playing it is a dinosaur

8. If we want to stop children from hitting one another, what should we call their hands?

A) Wild hands

B) Quiet hands

C) Gentle hands

QUESTIONS FOR THOUGHT

Write the answers to the following questions in a journal. Read through your answers at least once a week before you go to work.

1. Do you agree with the way Mario handled Alex and Jonah's argument? What did you like or dislike about it? How would you have handled it differently?
2. Has there been a situation at your job where you could have used the words *because, since, now that,* and *as long as* when explaining reasons, consequences, or causes/effects? Now, try to imagine future situations at your job that are similar to the examples given in this book.
3. Choose one or two new words that you just learned in the vocabulary section of this chapter and use them in conversation this week.
4. Record yourself repeating the sentences in the pronunciation section of this chapter. Listen to it. Do you think you sound confident and clear? What could you improve?
5. Do you agree with the advice given in the "Problems and Advice" reading section? What would you change or add to it? Ask a friend his or her opinion and have a discussion together.

GLOSSARY

- **to apologize**

(V) To say you are sorry

Example: *I **apologized** for losing my patience with her.*

- **a bad report**

(N) A negative summary of the day's events

Example: *No one wants their parents to hear a **bad report** of the day.*

- **a break**

(N) A rest from work

Example: *I am exhausted! I need to take **a break** now.*

- **to bribe**

(V) To offer a reward for good behavior

Example: *The young mother taught her child to use the toilet by **bribing** him with a piece of chocolate every time he went.*

- **to cool off**

(V) To take some time to calm down from anger or sadness

Example: *I am so angry! I need to **cool off**. I will be back soon.*

- **a concept**

(N) An idea

Example: *Do you understand the concept of what I am explaining to you?*

- **a consequence**

(N) A positive or negative effect of an action

Example: *When he threw his toy, it broke. Now he can't play with the toy anymore. That was the **consequence** of his action.*

- **disrespectful**

(Adj.) Rude or impolite

Example: *The student was **disrespectful** to the teacher, so she sent him to the principal's office.*

- **effective**

(Adj.) Working right; successful

Example: *I have found that using rewards and punishments is not a very* ***effective*** *way for me to discipline.*

- **to encourage**

(V) To give positive feedback so that someone continues to do something

Example: *His nanny always* ***encourages*** *him to study hard; he got an A on his report card.*

- **to escalate**

(V) To grow or get more serious

Example: *It started off as a small disagreement, but then it* ***escalated*** *into a huge fight.*

- **to facilitate**

(V) To lead an activity without teaching it

Example: *The au pair enjoys* ***facilitating*** *outdoor activities, so that the children learn by doing.*

- **permission**

(N) Approval to do something

Example: *I give you* ***permission*** *to eat one piece of chocolate after dinner.*

- **a picky eater**

(Adj. Phrase) A person who does not like to eat or try many different foods

Example: *My son is such a **picky eater**. He has about five meals he will eat; that's it.*

- **a play-date**

(N) A scheduled time for children to play with each other, arranged by their parents or caregivers

Example: *Are you free on Friday? Would you like to get the kids together for a **play-date** at my house?*

- **respectful**

(Adj.) Appropriate or polite

Example: *Your son is very **respectful**. He always speaks nicely to adults.*

- **a responsibility chart**

(N) A poster that shows children what chores or jobs they should complete

Example: *You are helping your family so much today! Look at all the stickers on your **responsibility chart.***

- **to share**

(V) To use the same toy or game at the same time without arguing about wanting to use it alone

Example: ***Share** the blocks. You can both help build one big tower.*

- **to grab**

(V) To aggressively take something without permission

Example: *He **grabbed** the sandwich right out of her hands.*

- **to solve**

(V) To fix a problem

Example: *He **solved** the fight by breaking the crayon in half, so both children could color with it.*

- **stubborn**

(Adj.) Not wanting to change your mind about something; determined in a negative way

Example: *She wanted only the blue crayon. She wouldn't agree to any other color. She can be very **stubborn** at times.*

- **a tantrum**

(N) Childish behavior that usually includes crying, yelling, throwing oneself on the floor, or sometimes hitting/kicking

Example: *The toddler was so tired from skipping his nap that he threw a **tantrum** when I turned off the TV.*

- **to yell**

(V) To raise your voice or speak very loudly

Note: Speakers of British English typically say 'shout' instead of 'yell.'

Example: *Don't **yell**. I know you are angry, but I am standing right here. I can hear you when you talk normally.*

CHAPTER 2 ANSWERS

Did You Understand?

1. His baseball

2. C) She will tell the boys' mother that they were misbehaving today.

3. "Cool off" - calm down, take a break, etc.

4. B) were a little bit stubborn, but soon made peace.

5. Outside

Language Point: Activity 1

1. C
2. E
3. A
4. B
5. G
6. H
7. D

8. F

Language Point: Activity 2 Possible Answers

1. sad + because + toy

She is sad because she wants to play with your toy.

2. tired + since + nap

Are you a little tired since you didn't nap today?

3. now that + friend + share

Now that your friend is here to play with you, don't forget to share with him.

4. as long as + finished + play

As long as he is finished with that crayon, you can color with it now.

Vocabulary Activity

1. facilitate 2. escalated 3. grabbed 4. tantrum 5. solve 6. consequence 7. encouraged 8. yelling 9. break 10. concept

Ideas for More Practice

Go to mindyourlanguage.us/audio-files/

Chapter 2 > More Practice

1 *Ideas 2-1*

Child: ***I'm tired.***

You: I'm sure you are. Would you like to take a short nap?

You: Aww, you've had a busy day. I'd be tired too, if I were you!

You: Perhaps you should go to bed a bit early tonight?

2 *Ideas 2-2*

Child: ***He started it!***

You: Now, now. Let's speak calmly please.

You: Can you use your indoor voice, please?

You: I will be happy to listen to you. I need you to speak a little quieter, though.

3 *Ideas* 2-3

Child: ***He took my baseball!***

You: No shouting. It's not okay to take someone else's things. He needs to wait his turn; please give it back.

You: Let's speak respectfully! He will give it back to you. It is not okay to take other people's things.

You: I know you're upset. Let's go tell him how you feel with a calm voice.

4 *Ideas* 2-4

Child: ***I can take the baseball whenever I want to since it was mine first.***

You: I'm sorry but that's not how it works.

You: Does that mean I can take back the Christmas presents I gave to you last month, since I bought them for you?

You: I do not appreciate the way you are speaking to me. Try telling me again how you feel, but with kinder words.

5 *Ideas* 2-5

Child: ***I don't care what you say to my mom.***

You: You don't mean that. Let's cool off now.

You: Take a break. Please go to your room for a few minutes.

You: Your mom wouldn't be happy to hear you saying those words. It's time for a little break now.

6 *Ideas 2-6*

Child: ***Give me my baseball! Now!***

You: We do not speak to each other like that.

You: I know you are upset, but there is no need to yell like that.

You: Try again. Start with the word "please" and lower your voice.

Reading

Activity 1

Problem 1 Advice C

Problem 2 Advice D

Problem 3 Advice E

Problem 4 Advice A

Problem 5 Advice B

Activity 2

1. B
2. B
3. C
4. B
5. B
6. A
7. A
8. C

CHAPTER 3: "WHAT'S YOUR HOMEWORK TODAY?"

HOW TO HELP CHILDREN WITH THEIR HOMEWORK

Sometimes it can be difficult to help children with their homework if English is not your first language.

The activities in Chapter 3 will teach you how to *understand* and *explain* homework directions, *assist* with assignments, and *motivate* children to do their work.

CONVERSATION

Read the conversation between Timothy and his au pair, Sean.

Sean: How was your day at school, today?

Timothy: It was fine. Nothing special.

Sean: Nothing special? I'm sure you learned something cool. What did you learn in science?

Timothy: Our teacher taught us about the solar system. We learned about the planets... like Jupiter!

Sean: That's SO cool.

Timothy: Yeah, it is pretty cool. She gave us a big homework project. But I don't have to do it tonight. It's due in two weeks.

Sean: Well, if you start it now, you won't have to do it all last minute. What's the project?

Timothy: We have to make a diorama. I need to look around the house for materials. We have a ping-pong ball, a cotton ball, a tennis ball...

Sean: That sounds SO cool. I bet if you paint the ping-pong ball blue and green, it will look just like Earth.

Timothy: I was already going to do that! If I attached fishing line to the balls, you won't be able to see the line and it will look like it's floating. Right?

Sean: Definitely. We can start it tonight. What about your math homework?

Timothy: I just have to study multiplication.

Sean: Okay. If you study with me before dinner, you will have time to start the diorama with me. We can work on it in the kitchen.

Timothy: Oh... I forgot. She gave me a worksheet, too. I don't really want to do it...

Sean: Timothy, you know that if you do your homework, you might receive a good grade on your report card.

Timothy: And if I get a good grade on my report card, my mom will buy me a new bicycle.

Sean: Exactly. So let's get started!

Listen to Chapter 3 Conversation 3.

Go to mindyourlanguage.us/audio-files/

Pause after you hear the au pair Sean and repeat his responses two to three times, until it feels natural. Do not read when you repeat. Look in a mirror instead.

DID YOU UNDERSTAND?

1. Which subject does Timothy prefer: science or math?

2. When is Timothy's Science project due?

   A) Tomorrow

   B) Next week

   C) In two weeks

3. What is Timothy planning to use for his model of Earth?

   A) A ping-pong ball

   B) A cotton ball

   C) A tennis ball

4. What does Timothy have for his math homework?

5. What will Timothy's mother buy him if he gets a good grade on his report card?

LANGUAGE POINT: CONDITIONS WITH "IF"

Using "if" helps us explain causes and effects.

This language point is useful when explaining homework

assignments, discussing time management, organizational skills, and good study habits with children.

Here are some examples.

If you add 5 and 2, you will get 7.

If + simple present + subject + will/won't…

If you study hard, you might get a good grade on the test.

If + simple present + subject + may/might…

If you finish your homework by 5: 00, you'll be able to play your videogames.

If + simple present + subject + will/won't be able to…

If you don't do your homework tonight, you'll have to do more work tomorrow.

If + simple present + subject + will/won't have to…

You can also reverse the order of clauses:

You might get a good grade on the test if you study hard.

Activity 1

Choose the best end for the sentences. The first one is done as an example.

1. If you do your best, you will succeed. (B)

    A) you will fail.

    B) you will succeed.

    C) you won't succeed.

    D) you can't succeed.

2. You might feel tired if

A) you go to sleep early.

B) you don't stay up late.

C) you stay up late.

D) you don't go to bed late.

3. You will be able to concentrate if

A) you study in a loud room.

B) you study in a quiet room.

C) you study in a messy room.

D) you don't study in a quiet room.

4. If you double-check your work,

A) you might miss a mistake.

B) you might make a lot of mistakes.

C) you might find and correct your mistakes.

D) you might forget your mistakes.

5. If you make flashcards,

A) you will be able to forget everything.

B) you will be able to remember nothing.

C) you won't be able to remember anything.

D) you will be able to remember a lot.

Activity 2

Create sentences by unscrambling the words and phrases below.

Remember to capitalize the first letter of a sentence and add punctuation, such as periods and commas.

Example: you stay up too late / at school tomorrow / if / you might feel tired / doing homework

Possible answer: You might feel tired at school tomorrow if you stay up too late doing homework.

1. you stay up too late / at school tomorrow / if / you might feel tired / doing homework
2. you do your best / if / on your homework / I will be proud of you
3. won't be able to read your work / your teacher / you don't write neatly / if
4. if / you will be able to / you study in a well-lit and quiet room / concentrate
5. make too many mistakes / double-check your work / if you / you might not
6. to memorize the facts / make flashcards / you will be able / if you

VOCABULARY

Look at these words. Which ones do you already know?

	I can use this word when I speak.	I know what this word means, but I don't use it.	I don't know this word.
a **diorama**			
creativity			
an **assignment**			
a **journal**			
a **cover**			
due			
rubric			
to **examine**			
to **post**			
FAQ			
to **click around**			

If you don't know some of these words, look them up in the glossary at the end of this chapter. Be sure you can use them when you speak.

Vocabulary Activity

Which words from the table belong in the blanks? The first one is done as an example.

Example: The homework is due on Friday.

1. The homework is ___________ on Friday.
2. The teacher ___________ a link to the video on her website. (*Hint: add -ed*)
3. The front ___________ of the catalogue showed photos of many children's books that I wanted to buy for him.
4. He made a ___________ in an old shoebox of a scene from his favorite book.
5. The website has a ___________ section that should help answer a lot of your concerns.
6. The pediatrician will ___________ her at her next checkup.
7. He has a wonderful imagination and strong sense of ___________.
8. The teacher gave him a very difficult ___________ and I am not sure he will be able to complete it by the deadline.

9. She writes in her ___________ every day.
10. Take a look at their website, and ___________ to see if you can find the information you need.

More Practice

Part 1: Read the questions that were seen in the conversation in the beginning of this chapter. How would you answer them in your own words? Write your answers down and practice saying them until it feels natural. (*Note: Do not listen to the audio files yet. This will happen in Part 2.*)

Example:

Timothy: *The teacher gave us a big homework project that's due in two weeks so I don't want to do it now.*

Possible idea ***You***: *I understand that. Why don't we go have a little snack and we can talk about some ideas while we eat?*

1. **Timothy**: The teacher gave us a big homework project that's due in 2 weeks so I don't want to do it now. (*Chapter 3, Ideas 3-1*)

You:

2. **Timothy**: We have to make a diorama. Will it look cool if I paint the ping-pong ball blue and green, like Earth? (*Chapter 3, Ideas 3-2*)

You:

3. **Timothy**: How can I make the planets look like they are floating? (*Chapter 3, Ideas 3-3*)

You:

4. **Timothy**: Do I have to do my math homework before dinner? (*Chapter 3, Ideas 3-4*)

You:

5. **Timothy**: I don't really want to do my homework right now. I can still get a good grade without doing my homework, right? (*Chapter* 3, *Ideas* 3-5)

You:

6. **Timothy**: Mom said she wanted my grades to improve so she could buy me a bicycle. (*Chapter* 3, *Ideas* 3-6)

You:

Part 2: Go to mindyourlanguage.us/audio-files/ and listen to each question. Pause the audio after the question is asked, and answer it in your own words. Then, restart the audio to hear more ways you could answer Timothy. Repeat these example answers until it feels natural to you.

PRONUNCIATION

Activity 1

Read the words and phrases aloud. Then listen to them and repeat.

Go to mindyourlanguage.us/audio-files/

Chapter 3 > Pronunciation > Activity 1 > Pronunciation 3

What did you learn? | last minute | math homework
study with me | work on it | good grade | get started

Activity 2

Listen to the sentences and repeat them aloud. Try practicing the sentences in different ways so that you can use them naturally and confidently in your job.

Go to mindyourlanguage.us/audio-files/

Chapter 3 > Pronunciation > Activity 2

1. What did you learn in history class today?

2. Let's not wait until last minute to start your project.
3. You don't want to wait to do it all last minute, do you?
4. What do you have tonight for your math homework?
5. Have you studied your multiplication facts for your math homework?
6. Would you like to study with me?
7. It will be more fun if you study with me.
8. Let's work on it together.
9. I am sure you will earn a good grade if you work hard on the assignment.
10. Let's get started on your Stargazing Journal.

READING

"Stargazing Journal"

Read the homework assignment from Timothy's teacher.

Have you seen this type of assignment before?

Dear Class,

Your solar system dioramas last week were incredible! I am so proud of your hard work and creativity. Isn't space cool?! This week, you are going to become astronomers. Watch out NASA... here comes Ms. Brummer's super scientists!

Your assignment is to create a STARGAZING JOURNAL. Every night, you will go outside with your "assistant astronomer" (your parent or guardian), and you will answer the following questions about the night sky:

What's the date?

Where are you located?

How's the weather?

Do you see any constellations in the sky?

Then, at the bottom of the page, you will draw a picture of everything you see in the sky. Your picture should be at least 5 inches by 5 inches. Don't forget to draw things you see while looking up, such as trees or rooftops.

You will do this every night for one week. So, your stargazing journal will be 7 pages long. Please also include a front cover. If you start tonight, May 16, you will be able to finish by Friday, May 20. The finished project is due next Monday, May 23.

I have posted examples of this assignment on my website. I have also posted the rubric I will be using to grade it. Be sure to examine the rubric closely so you know what I will be looking for. Finally, I have posted some FAQs about the assignment with their answers. If you still have a question after clicking around my website, you'll have to ask me in school!

I can't wait to see your amazing Stargazing Journals!

~Ms. Brummer

Activity 1

Answer the questions below, based on the reading.

1. What is the homework assignment this week?

   A) A diorama

   B) Watching NASA on TV

   C) A Stargazing Journal

2. What is a Stargazing Journal?

A) A book report homework assignment

B) Nightly observations about the sky and its surroundings

C) An online newspaper

3. What does NOT need to be included in the assignment?

A) Any sounds heard

B) Description of the weather

C) Any constellations seen

4. How big should the illustrations be drawn?

A) Half a page

B) A quarter of a page

C) 5" x 5"

5. Which of the following should not be included in the illustrations?

A) Grass

B) Treetops

C) Skylines

6. When is the assignment's deadline?

A) May 16

B) May 20

C) May 23

7. What is NOT posted on Ms. Brummer's website?

A) A grading rubric

B) Photos of the sky

C) Common questions

8. What should the students do if they have questions after reading the website?

A) Ask the teacher

B) Ask a friend

C) Ask a parent

QUESTIONS FOR THOUGHT

Write the answers to the following questions in a journal. Read through your answers at least once a week before you go to work.

1. How did the au pair encourage Timothy to discuss more details about his day at school? How did he encourage him to get started on his homework assignments? Would you do this in similar style or differently?
2. Do you often hear conditions with 'if'? Which examples given in this book could you use in your job? Which examples would feel most natural for you to use?
3. Choose one or two new words that you just learned in the vocabulary section of this chapter and use them in conversation this week.
4. Record yourself repeating the sentences in the pronunciation section of this chapter. Listen to it. Do you think you sound confident and clear? What could you work on?
5. Would you feel comfortable helping Timothy with his Stargazing Journal homework assignment? Were any parts

of the teacher's letter unclear? How would you ask the teacher for more information?

GLOSSARY

- **an assignment**

(N) A piece of work given to complete, especially in school

Example: *Joseph worked hard to get an A on his* ***assignment****.*

- **an astronomer**

(N) A person who studies stars and planets

Example: *In the 1500s,* ***an astronomer*** *named Copernicus said that the earth went around the sun.*

- **to click around**

(V Phrase) To browse or look through a website

Example: *Beatrice* ***clicked around*** *a few websites until she found a good one.*

- **a checkup**

(N) A health examination

Example: *Jamie took her children to the doctor for regular* ***checkups***.

- **to concentrate**

(V) To focus or pay close attention

Example: *Andy always studied in the library because it helped him* ***concentrate***.

- **a constellation**

(N) Stars grouped together to make a shape

Example: *I love looking up at the stars and finding* ***constellations*** *like the Big Dipper.*

- **creativity**

(N) Imagination; original thought

Example: *Jane had a* ***creative*** *idea that evening. Instead of watching TV she drew pictures.*

- **a deadline**

(N) The date and time something must be done

Example: *The teacher said that the homework must be handed in by the* ***deadline***.

- **a diorama**

(N) A model exhibit

Example: *The librarian decorated her library with **dioramas** of animals in forest scenes.*

- **due**

(Adj.) When something should or must happen

Example: *The assignment is **due** on Friday.*

- **to examine**

(V) Study; investigate in detail

Example: *The young child **examined** the shell she found on the beach.*

- **to fail**

(V) To receive the worst grade

Example: *Joan was sad that she **failed** the test. Next time, she will study harder.*

- **FAQs**

(N) Frequently Asked Questions

Example: *The teacher asked her students to read the **FAQs** before asking questions.*

- **a fishing line**

(N) A thin clear line used to catch a fish

Example: *In my classroom, I hang art projects from the ceiling with **fishing line.***

- **flashcards**

(N) Cards with facts written on them, to help with studying

Example: *I got an A on the assignment because I remembered all the **flashcards** I had made.*

- **to float**

(V) To rest or move in water or air

Example: *The clouds **float** in the sky beautifully.*

- **the cover**

(N) The outside part of a book

Example: *The front **cover** of this book has a nanny on it.*

- **the last minute**

(N) The time right before something happens

Example: *Don't wait until **the last minute** to start studying. Do a little bit each day.*

- **a journal**

(N) A record of everyday events; a diary

Example: *I write down what I do every day in my **journal**.*

- **Jupiter**

(N) A large planet that is fifth from the sun

Example: ***Jupiter*** *is the most interesting planet in the solar system.*

- **an illustration**

(N) A drawing

Example: *The artist's job is to draw* ***illustrations*** *for children's books.*

- **an inch**

(N) A unit of measure

Example: *The white paper is 8 ½ by 11* ***inches***.

- **a model**

(N) A version of something, often smaller

Example: *The tiny* ***model*** *of an airplane shows all the parts of a real airplane.*

- **NASA**

(N) National Aeronautics and Space Administration

Example: *My cousin is an astronaut who works for* ***NASA***.

- **neatly**

(Adv.) In a tidy, clean way

Example: *Please put all your toys away* ***neatly*** *before we go on our bike ride.*

- **ping-pong**

(N) Table tennis

Example: *My favorite Olympic sport is **ping-pong**!*

- **to post**

(V) To write and publish something on the internet, particularly on social media

Example: *Did you see what she **posted**? I can't believe she put that picture online.*

- **a report card**

(N) A paper that shows all the grades a student receives for a certain amount of time

Example: *Her **report card** was great! She got all A's.*

- **a rooftop**

(N) The top of a building's roof

Example: *The snow settled on the **rooftop**. It looks very beautiful.*

- **a rubric**

(N) A guide that shows what teachers expect on an assignment

Example: *Our writing assignment's **rubric** included spelling, grammar, punctuation, style, and ideas.*

- **a skyline**

(N) The outline of buildings and trees against the sky

Example: *The New York City **skyline** is beautiful because of its many tall buildings.*

- **the solar system**

(N) The eight planets and moons around our sun

Example: *He loves his science class because they are learning about the **solar system**.*

- **to stargaze**

(V) To look at the night sky and enjoy the stars

Example: *Sometimes after a hard day, it helps to sit outside and **stargaze**.*

- **to succeed**

(V) To achieve goals

Example: *You did it! You won the contest. You **succeeded** in your goal. Congratulations!*

- **time management**

(N) an understanding of how the day is spent and the scheduling of tasks in order to be more organized

Example: *I decided to stop checking my social media this month to help me with my **time management**.*

CHAPTER 3 ANSWERS

Did You Understand?

1. Science

2. C

3. A

4. He has to study his multiplication facts.

5. A bicycle

Language Point: Part 1

1. B
2. C
3. B
4. C
5. D

Language Point: Part 2

1. You might feel tired at school tomorrow if you stay up too late doing homework. *–or–*If you stay up too late doing homework, you might feel tired at school tomorrow.
2. If you do your best on your homework, I will be proud of you. *–or–* I will be proud of you if you do your best on your homework.
3. If you don't write neatly, your teacher won't be able to read your work. *–or–* Your teacher won't be able to read your work if you don't write neatly.
4. If you study in a well-lit and quiet room, you will be able to concentrate. *–or–* You will be able to concentrate if you study in a well-lit and quiet room.
5. If you double-check your work, you might not make too many mistakes. *–or–* You might not make too many mistakes if you double-check your work.
6. If you make flashcards, you will be able to remember a lot. *–or–* You will be able to remember a lot if you make flashcards.

Vocabulary Activity

1. due
2. posted
3. front cover
4. diorama
5. FAQs
6. examine
7. creativity
8. assignment
9. journal
10. click around

Ideas for More Practice

Go to mindyourlanguage.us/audio-files/

Chapter 3 > More Practice

1 *Ideas 3-1*

Timothy: My day at school today was fine. We learned about the solar system in science. The teacher gave us a big homework project that's due in 2 weeks so I don't want to do it now.

You: You know, if you do a little bit each day, it will make it easier in the long run.

You: You don't have to do it RIGHT now. How about we play together for 20 minutes and then do a little bit of planning?

You: I'll make you a deal. We can play basketball for 15 minutes and then work on the project for 15 minutes. Sound good?

2 *Ideas 3-2*

Timothy: We have to make a diorama. Will it look cool if I paint the ping-pong ball blue and green, like Earth?

You: How creative! I think that would look really good.

You: Sounds awesome! I like your creativity.

You: I think that would look a lot like Earth. Let's do that.

3 *Ideas 3-3*

Timothy: How can I make the planets look like they are floating?

You: We could attach a fishing line to the balls. What do you think?

You: Why don't we stick the balls to clear line?

You: Let's attach some fishing line to the balls. Do you think that would work?

4 *Ideas 3-4*

Timothy: Do I have to do my math homework before dinner?

You: That would be a good idea. Then we could start the science project later.

You: You can choose. Would you rather do your math homework or get started on the science project first?

You: I think that would be the best way to manage your time. Do you agree?

5 *Ideas 3-5*

Timothy: I don't really want to do my homework right now. I can still get a good grade without doing my homework, right?

You: Sorry, Timothy. In life, there are no shortcuts.

You: Working hard is the only way to get ahead.

You: Nope! Homework is part of your grade, you know.

6 *Ideas 3-6*

Timothy: Mom said she wanted my grades to improve so she could buy me a bicycle.

You: You must work hard, Timothy!

You: You are a very bright young man. Let's work hard so you can get that bicycle.

You: I bet you would love riding a bike around the park with me. Let's go study!

Reading

1. C

2. B
3. A
4. C
5. A
6. B
7. A

CHAPTER 4: "WHAT DO YOU WANT FOR DINNER?"

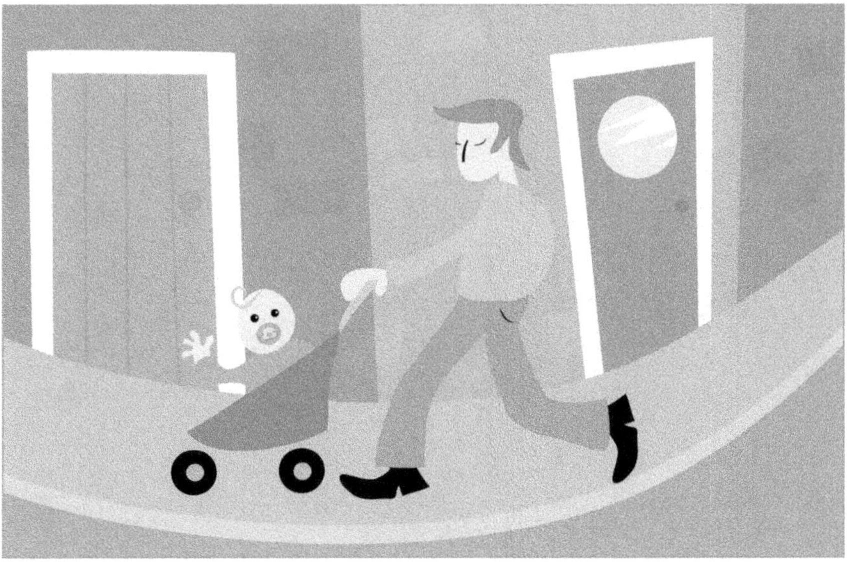

HOW TO TALK ABOUT FOOD

Eating is a universal language, but talking about it is not!

When you are watching a child, food is a very important topic.

The activities in Chapter 4 will teach you all about food: how to deal with *fussy eaters*, vocabulary related to *food allergies*, and ways to give *food suggestions*.

CONVERSATION

Read the conversation between Brittany and her babysitter, Alan.

Brittany: Let's have dinner soon. I'm starving!

Alan: Okay. What are you in the mood for?

Brittany: Well, I don't want chicken. We have had chicken too much this week.

Alan: You're right. Well, we should have a different meat for protein.

Brittany: Okay… could we have hot dogs for dinner?

Alan: We could. But that's not really that healthy. Why don't you choose a different meat for tonight?

Brittany: Okay… hamburgers?

Alan: Come on.

Brittany: Okay, okay. We should have steak teriyaki!

Alan: Great. Let's go defrost the steak from the freezer, and then you could help me marinate it with the teriyaki sauce.

Brittany: Okay. What else?

Alan: Well, we should have a carb and a vegetable.

Brittany: What's a carb?

Alan: A carbohydrate. Like potatoes, bread, rice…

Brittany: Let's have rice for the carb. And broccoli for the vegetable.

Alan: Sounds perfect. Your mom will be so proud of you for choosing such a healthy dinner to eat.

LISTEN TO CHAPTER 4 Conversation 4. Go to:

mindyourlanguage.us/audio-files/

Pause after you hear the babysitter and repeat his responses two-three times, until it feels natural. Do not read when you repeat. Look in a mirror instead.

DID YOU UNDERSTAND?

1. Why doesn't Brittany want to eat chicken for dinner?

    A) She is a vegetarian.

    B) She is sick of eating chicken this week.

    C) She doesn't like chicken.

2. Why did the babysitter say no to hot dogs?

    A) Hot dogs are unhealthy.

    B) They don't have any hot dogs in the house.

    C) He doesn't like hot dogs.

3. What did they decide to make for dinner?

4. What did they choose for the carb?

    A) potatoes

    B) bread

    C) rice

5. What did they choose for the vegetable?

LANGUAGE POINT: SUGGESTIONS

Let's, ***Why don't*** ... ?, ***could***, and ***should*** are used to give suggestions. In this chapter, we will focus on suggestions in the context of food.

Look at the examples below:

Modal	What it means
Let's...	A suggestion for us
Why don't [we/you/I]... ?	Casual suggestion(s) – *(Remember the question mark.)*
[You/We/I] could...	Optional suggestion(s)
[You/We/I] should...	Strong suggestion(s)

Activity 1

Match the beginnings to their correct endings.

***Example**: Why don't we have shrimp for dinner?* **(D)**

1. Why don't we	**A)** You could help me make a nice big salad to accompany the chicken.
2. I'm in the mood for Japanese food. Let's	**B)** It will make you get over your cold.
3. Why don't we cook some chicken legs?	**C)** have sushi with soy sauce.
4. We should have a barbecue tonight.	**D)** have some shrimp for dinner?
5. If you behave tonight,	**E)** or a peanut butter and jelly sandwich, if you want. It's up to you.
6. We should have a vegetable stir-fry tonight for dinner.	**F)** let's go out for ice cream. I know that's your favorite dessert.
7. You could have an egg and cheese omelet.	**G)** We could have hamburgers and hot dogs.
8. We should have a nice healthy chicken soup tonight	**H)** I know you like the baby corn! What other veggies should we add to it?

Activity 2

Create your own sentences using the given words.

Example Question: let's + pizza

Possible Answer *"Let's order pizza tonight."*

1. let's + pizza

2. should + Chinese food

3. could + barbecue

4. why don't + go out

VOCABULARY

Look at these words. Which ones do you already know?

	I can use this word when I speak.	I know what this word means, but I don't use it.	I don't know this word.
baby-led weaning			
strategy			
an aspect			
bribe			
assist			
explore			
pretend			
a phase			
nutrients			
choke			

If you don't know some of these words, look them up in the glossary at the end of this chapter. Be sure you can use them when you speak.

Vocabulary Activity

Which words from the table belong in the blanks? The first one is done as an example.

1. He is going through a *phase* where he only wants to eat peanut butter and jelly sandwiches!
2. Let's ___________ that we are dinosaurs eating giant trees!
3. The young child loves to ___________ new food by touching, smelling, and playing with it.
4. The mother is worried her child is not getting enough

___________, so she makes him take a vitamin every morning.

5. The best ___________ to get him to follow directions is to make it into a game.
6. Sometimes, the only way to get Sally to get dressed quickly is to ___________ her with a sticker.
7. It is very important to cut food into small pieces so that the child does not ___________!
8. Try to avoid ___________ the child in eating. If he can do it by himself, he should do it by himself. (*Hint: add -ing*)
9. Instead of blending the food into mush, why don't you try ___________?
10. There are so many ___________ to a nanny's job! (*Hint: add -s*)

More Practice

Part 1: Read the questions that were seen in the conversation in the beginning of this chapter. How would you answer them in your own words? Write your answers down and practice saying them until it feels natural. (Note: Do not listen to the audio files yet. This will happen in Part 2.)

Example:

Brian: *Let's have dinner soon. I'm starving!*

Possible idea *You: Me too. We could have some leftovers from yesterday. How does that sound?*

1. **Brian**: Let's have dinner soon. I'm starving! (*Chapter 4, Ideas 4-1*)

You:

2. **Brian**: Well, I don't want chicken. (*Chapter 4, Ideas 4-2*)

You:

3. **Brian**: Could we have hot dogs for dinner? (*Chapter* 4, *Ideas* 4-3)

You:

4. **Brian**: We should have steak teriyaki! (*Chapter* 4, *Ideas* 4-4)

You:

5. **Brian**: Okay, what else? (*Chapter* 4, *Ideas* 4-5)

You:

6. **Brian**: What's a carb? (*Chapter* 4, *Ideas* 4-6)

You:

7. **Brian**: Let's have rice for the carb. And broccoli for the vegetable.

(*Chapter* 4, *Ideas* 4-7)

You:

Part 2: Go to mindyourlanguage.us/audio-files/ and listen to each question. Pause the audio after the question is asked, and answer it in your own words. Then, restart the audio to hear more ways you could respond to Brian. Repeat these example responses until they feel natural to you.

PRONUNCIATION

Activity 1

Read the words and phrases aloud. Then listen to them at mindyourlanguage.us/audio-files/ *and repeat.*

Chapter 4 > Pronunciation > Activity 1 > Pronunciation 4

starving | in the mood for | protein
defrost it | marinate it | healthy

Activity 2

Listen to the sentences and repeat them aloud. Try practicing the sentences in different ways so that you can use them naturally and confidently in your job.

Go to mindyourlanguage.us/audio-files/

Chapter 4 > Pronunciation > Activity 2

1. You haven't eaten all day. You must be starving!

2. I'm starving! What do we have in the fridge?
3. I'm in the mood for something vegetarian tonight.
4. If you don't want to eat meat, make sure you have a different kind of protein.
5. I have some salmon in the freezer. Let's defrost it.
6. I want to make it tomorrow. I will put it in the fridge to defrost it overnight.
7. What should we use to marinate it?
8. This meal is so healthy. Your parents will be so happy.
9. You can only have one more cookie. It is not very healthy.
10. Make a healthy choice.

READING

Dealing with Fussy Eaters

Part 1: Read the paragraphs and then match the headings to each paragraph. The first one is done as an example.

Headings

A) Choices, Choices, Choices

B) Kids Can Help Prepare

C) Let It Be

D) Bribes Might Work

E) Let the Baby Explore!

F) Make it Fun

It is very common for children to be fussy when it comes to eating. Here are some tips that may help encourage children to try eating new things.

Paragraph 1. ______________________________

When children are as young as six months, they can start developing a healthy relationship with food. "Baby-led weaning" is a great way to do this. Give the child pieces of soft food like avocado or banana, and let them play with it. Let them explore the food and make a mess. It doesn't matter if they eat much of the food at this age. If they can play with the food, smell it, and lick it off their fingers, it is a success! (Be sure the pieces of food are soft so there is no risk of choking.)

Paragraph 2. ______________________________

Letting children assist with food shopping and cooking is a wonderful way to make them feel like they are in control of the food they eat. If you are able to take them to the grocery store, why don't you let them touch and explore the fruits and vegetables that you put in the shopping cart? Children of all ages love to participate in the cooking process. Mixing, spreading, and adding spices are really fun activities!

Paragraph 3. ______________________________

It helps to have a variety of food on the table so that the children could have a choice. For example, you could have two options of vegetables on the table and ask the child to choose one of them. It also helps if they watch you eat both vegetables. The more they see other people eating something, the more likely they are to want to try it.

Paragraph 4. ______________________________

Playing games with young children is a fun way to encourage them to try new foods. You could pretend that chicken soup is a "laughing soup," and whenever you take a bite, it makes you laugh! You could pretend to be a monkey eating a banana, making monkey noises as you eat the food. It is always fun to play games, isn't it? Let's be silly!

Paragraph 5. ______________________________

Some parents insist that the only thing that works for their children is bribery! For a child who only wants to eat peanut butter crackers, perhaps you should let them have a peanut butter cracker for every three bites he takes of his dinner. This way, he will be motivated to eat the new food, he will still get what he wants, and you can feel better knowing he is getting nutrients into his body!

Paragraph 6. ____

When all else fails, like John Lennon says: "Let it be." Many pediatricians say that children know which nutrients their body needs. Sometimes, kids go through phases of only wanting one particular food all the time. As long as they are gaining weight and growing, there is really no need to stress too much about it.

Part 2: *Answer the questions below, based on the reading.*

1. Why is it so important to give soft foods when you are using the "baby-led weaning" technique?

A. The baby could choke

B. The baby won't like hard foods

C. The baby only likes avocados and bananas

2. At what age do children grow out of being picky eaters?

A. 4

B. 7

C. Not given

3. Which is NOT a suggested game to try?

A. Pretending to a monkey

B. Pretending that soup is freezing cold

C. Pretending that soup makes you laugh

4. Why do children love to be involved in the cooking process?

A. They love to mix, spread, and add spices

B. It makes them feel like they are in control of what they eat

C. Both A and B

5. What is the most important thing for parents and nannies to understand about children's eating habits?

A. Most children go through phases where they love to eat all foods.

B. Most children do not enjoy eating.

C. As long as children are growing and gaining weight, they are most likely okay.

6. Does bribery help children try new foods?

A. Always

B. Sometimes

C. Never

7. What is the goal of baby-led weaning?

A. For the baby to play with the food and explore it

B. For the baby to finish his meal

C. For the baby to make a mess

8. When children watch other people eating something,

A. they are likely to want to try it.

B. they probably won't want to try it.

C. they might not want to try it.

QUESTIONS FOR THOUGHT

Write the answers to the following questions in a journal. Read through your answers at least once a week before you go to work.

1. What do you think about the way the babysitter discussed dinner options with Brittany? Would you have let her help make the decision? Would you have tried to convince her to eat chicken again? Would you have agreed to hot dogs or hamburgers? How would you have expressed your ideas in English?
2. Do you often give meal suggestions using the words *let's, could, should,* and *why don't...?* Besides food, what other situations could you imagine using these words and phrases?
3. Choose one or two new words that you just learned in the vocabulary section of this chapter and use them in conversation this week.
4. Record yourself repeating the sentences in the pronunciation section of this chapter. Listen to it. Do you think you sound confident and clear? What could you work on?
5. What other strategies might help fussy eaters to try new foods?

GLOSSARY

- **an aspect**

(N) a part of something bigger

Example: *My favorite* ***aspect*** *of my job is reading Danny his favorite bedtime stories before he goes to bed.*

- **to assist**

(V) to help with something

Example: *Could you please* ***assist*** *me with this stroller? I don't know how to close it!*

- **baby-led weaning**

(N Phrase) a style of feeding babies that gives them soft solid foods at an early age, and skips blending the foods.

Example: *I think my daughter is a great eater because we let her practice Baby-Led Weaning when she started eating.*

- **to bribe**

(V) to offer a reward for a good behavior or good choice

Example: *Every time he used the toilet, I* ***bribed*** *him with a small "potty prize." Soon, he was out of diapers.*

- **carbohydrates**

(N) A type of food that contains sugar and starch

Example: *I get very hungry unless I eat* ***carbohydrates*** *with my meals.*

- **to choke**

(V) To have trouble breathing because food or an item gets stuck in the throat

Example: *The boy* ***choked****, so I did the Heimlich Maneuver.*

- **to defrost**

(V) to go from frozen to room temperature

Example: *Let's* ***defrost*** *the meat so we can cook it later.*

- **to explore**

(V) to learn about something in detail by using sight, smell, taste, etc.

Example: *She wanted to* ***explore*** *the new toy I gave to her. She spent 45 minutes taking it apart and putting it back together.*

- **fish sticks**

(N) Pieces of fried fish - a children's meal

Example: *Would you like some* ***fish sticks*** *with your green beans?*

- **to gain**

(V) to increase something, like weight

Example: *I* ***gained*** *5 pounds after Christmas break.*

- **to marinate**

(V) To soak food in liquid before cooking or eating

Example: *Let's* ***marinate*** *the fish in soy sauce.*

- **a nutrient**

(N) a substance found in food that helps people stay healthy

Example: *I feel so good after eating this salad. There are so many* ***nutrients*** *in it!*

- **an omelet**

(N) An egg meal

Example: *Would you like an* ***omelet*** *for breakfast? I can put some onions and peppers in it, or you could have it plain if you like.*

- **a phase**

(N) A period of time where changes take place in one's development

Example: *She is going through a* ***phase*** *where she wants to carry her teddy bear everywhere she goes.*

- **picky**

(Adj.) To want to eat or do only specific things

Example: *My son is* ***picky****. He won't eat fish, vegetables, or cheese.*

- **to pretend**

(V) To speak and act like someone or something different than yourself, while playing

Example: *Let's* ***pretend****! You can be the prince and I will be the princess.*

- **protein**

(N) A dietary substance found in meat, beans, and other food

Example: *My mother always tells me to make sure I am eating* ***protein*** *with my meals.*

- **on a regular basis**

(Adj. phrase) **Something that happens routinely, or commonly**

Example: *He enjoys going to the park* ***on a regular basis****, as long as the weather is good.*

- **a responsibility**

(N) The state of good decisions being made; when someone is accountable for something

Example: *Taking good care of these children is my **responsibility**.*

- **starving**

(Adj.) Extremely hungry

Example: *He said he was **starving**, so I gave him some yogurt while I finished making dinner.*

- **stir-fry**

(V) **To fry meat and vegetables while stirring**

Example: *I want to try the delicious Asian **stir-fry** that my cousin told me about.*

- **strategy**

(N) A plan of action

Example: *A good **strategy** for avoiding temper tantrums is to give the child a 5 minute warning before cleaning up or turning off the TV.*

- **teriyaki sauce**

(N) A Japanese sauce made of soy sauce, ginger, garlic, and other ingredients

Example: *My cousin loves **teriyaki sauce**, so I always cook with it when she comes over.*

- **a vegetarian**

(N) A person who does not eat meat

Example: *My brother has been a **vegetarian** ever since he watched a documentary about meat.*

- **veggies**

(N) Informal for vegetables

Example: *Don't forget to eat your **veggies**!*

CHAPTER 4 ANSWERS

Did You Understand?

1. B
2. A
3. Steak teriyaki
4. C
5. broccoli

Language Point: Activity 1

1. D
2. C
3. A
4. G
5. F
6. H
7. E
8. B

Language Point: Activity 2 Possible Answers

1. let's + pizza

Let's order pizza tonight.

2. should + Chinese food

We should get Chinese food for dinner.

3. could + barbecue

We could barbecue some hamburgers for dinner.

4. why don't + go out

Why don't we go out for lunch today?

Vocabulary Activity

1. phase

2. pretend

3. explore

4. nutrients

5. strategy

6. bribe

7. choke

8. assisting

9. baby-led weaning

10. aspects

Ideas for More Practice

Go to mindyourlanguage.us/audio-files/

Chapter 4 > More Practice

1 *Ideas 4-1*

Brian: *Let's have dinner soon. I'm starving!*

You: Me too. What would you like tonight?

You: Okay, what should we make?

You: Can you have some carrot sticks to hold you over until dinner time? It will be served in 30 minutes.

2 *Ideas 4-2*

Brian: *Well, I don't want chicken.*

You: Me neither. What meat would you like tonight?

You: Okay, no chicken. Do you want fish or red meat?

You: Fair enough. No chicken tonight. Let's look in the freezer for something else.

3 *Ideas 4-3*

Brian: *Could we have hot dogs for dinner?*

You: I'm not really in the mood for hot dogs. Can we have something a little healthier tonight?

You: Perhaps. I wonder if there's other options. Let's look and see.

You: I suppose we could, if there's nothing else. I am not really a fan of hot dogs. Is there anything else you'd like instead?

4 *Ideas 4-4*

Brian: *We should have steak teriyaki!*

You: Mmmmm I love that idea. Let's get started.

You: Yum! Okay, let's make it.

You: You read my mind! Steak teriyaki it is.

5 *Ideas 4-5*

Brian: *Okay. What else?*

You: Potatoes or rice? And what kind of vegetable would you like?

You: We have some sweet potatoes in the fridge. Do you want to make a salad?

You: Are you in the mood for soup or salad?

6 *Ideas 4-6*

Brian: *What's a carb?*

You: It's short for carbohydrate.

You: Bread, rice, potatoes... things that make you stay full for longer.

You: Things like pasta or potatoes. They keep you feeling full.

7 *Ideas 4-7*

Brian: *Let's have rice for the carb. And broccoli for the vegetable.*

You: Okay, wonderful. Let's get started then.

You: All right. I like the sound of that. Let's make it.

You: Okay, this is going to be a delicious meal!

Reading

Activity 1

A) Paragraph 3

B) Paragraph 2

C) Paragraph 6

D) Paragraph 5

E) Paragraph 1

F) Paragraph 4

Activity 2

1. A
2. C
3. B
4. C
5. C
6. B
7. A
8. A

CHAPTER 5: "OW, I HURT MYSELF!"

HOW TO USE BASIC MEDICAL ENGLISH

Any parent or guardian of a child will tell you that health and safety is, by far, the most important thing when it comes to watching children.

The activities in Chapter 5 teach you all about what to do in case a child is *sick*, *injured*, *feeling discomfort*, or in need of *medical attention*.

CONVERSATIONS

Read the short conversations. There are five different ones.

Conversation 1

Stella: My face hurts. Look at it! It's so red, it burns.

Nanny: Were you out in the sun today?

Stella: Yes!

Nanny: It's a sunburn. Let's put some lotion on it, okay? It will help it feel cooler. I will text your mom now.

Conversation 2

Doctor: What's the problem?

Au Pair: Ricky can't breathe! What should I do?

Doctor: Ricky has severe asthma. It is an asthma attack. Give him two puffs of his inhaler and we will send an ambulance immediately.

Conversation 3

Pediatrician: What does Stacy's rash look like?

Nanny: There are red bumps all over her arms and legs.

Pediatrician: What food did she eat today? Anything unusual?

Nanny: She had shrimp, but she has eaten shrimp before and never had a problem.

Pediatrician: Well, it might be an allergic reaction. Please bring her into my office so I can look at it.

Conversation 4

Ricky: *Ah-choo!* I don't feel so good.

Nanny: Oh, sweetie, it could be a cold. Let's sit down in front of the TV for a little bit, okay? I will give your dad a call.

Liam: Okay.

Nanny: I want you to drink some orange juice. You need to have a lot of fluid if you want to get better. I'll have a glass, too.

Conversation 5

Anna: I can't drink anything! It will make me feel sick!

Nanny: I know you don't want it, but just take small sips for me, okay? Your body needs to liquids. How about some water?

Anna: No!

Nanny: I know it's uncomfortable. Here, just a tiny sip. You drink five small sips. Then you can watch TV while I call your mommy.

Listen to Chapter 5 Conversations 1 through 5:

mindyourlanguage.us/audio-files/

Pause after you hear the nanny or au pair and repeat their responses two-three times, until it feels natural. Do not read when you repeat. Look in a mirror instead.

DID YOU UNDERSTAND?

1. What did the nanny do for Stella's sunburn?

    A) Call the hospital.

    B) Put some lotion on it and contact the parents.

    C) Put ice on it and contact the parents.

2. What did the doctor advise for Ricky's asthma attack?

A) Give him his inhaler.

B) Let him breathe into a paper bag.

C) Tell him to relax.

3. What did the pediatrician advise for Stacy's rash?

A) Give her a painkiller.

B) Give her an antihistamine and an oatmeal bath.

C) Come to the pediatrician's office.

4. What did the nanny do for Ricky's cold?

A) Let him relax and make him drink lots of fluids.

B) Give him hot tea with lemon.

C) Give him cold and flu medicine.

5. What did the nanny do for Anna's stomach virus?

A) Keep her hydrated and call her parents.

B) Rub her stomach and sing her songs.

C) Give her soda.

LANGUAGE POINT: MODALS & ADVERBS

We can use **modals** and **adverbs** when we talk about the children's health. Look at the examples below:

	Modals	Adverbs
100% -->	It **must** be the flu.	It is **definitely** the flu.
75% -->	It **could** be the flu.	It is **probably** the flu.
50% -->	It **might** be the flu.	**Maybe** it is the flu.

Activity 1

Match the first part of the sentence to the part that fits best.

Example: Stella's face is very red and sore. It could be a sunburn. (D)

1) Stella's face is very red and sore. It could	**A)** be an allergic reaction.
2) Ricky can't breathe. It is definitely	**B)** probably a cold.
3) Stacy has a rash. It might	**C)** an asthma attack.
4) Liam is coughing and sneezing. It is	**D)** be a sunburn.
5) Stella's face is burning. It is	**E)** be an asthma attack.
6) Ricky can't catch his breath. It must	**F)** probably a sunburn.
7) Stacy has bumps all over her arms and legs. Maybe it	**G)** be a cold.
8) Liam doesn't feel so good. He keeps sneezing. It could	**H)** is an allergic reaction.

Activity 2

Create your own sentences using the words given.

Example: Abigail + headache + probably + dehydrated

Possible idea: Abigail has a headache. She is probably dehydrated. Let's get her something to drink.

1. Abigail + headache + probably + dehydrated

2. Daniel + fever + might + virus

3. David + stomach pains + maybe + food poisoning

4. Lilly's ears + red + could + sunburn

VOCABULARY

Look at these words. Which ones do you already know?

	I can use this word when I speak.	**I know what this word means, but I don't use it.**	**I don't know this word.**
first aid			
symptoms			
a **stuffy nose**			
a **body ache**			
an **earache**			
protection			
hydrated			
dust			
pollen			
anxiety			
trigger			

Vocabulary Activity

Which words from the table belong in the blanks? The first one is done as an example.

1. He has a *stuffy nose,* so he has been snoring a lot at night. We need to buy more tissues!
2. Be sure to drink a lot of water so you stay ___________ in this heat.

3. The ___________ from the flowers outside is making my eyes water.
4. When he started coughing, it ___________ an asthma attack. (*Hint: add -ed*)
5. The flu gave me a full ___________. I couldn't leave my bed for a week.
6. When she was studying for her test, she started to feel some ___________. I told her to take a break to calm down.
7. Some ___________ of a cold are: runny nose, coughing, and sneezing.
8. Make sure you carry a ___________ kit in case of emergency that contains bandages, creams, tweezers, and rubber gloves.
9. When we opened the attic door, the first thing we noticed was a lot of ___________. We all started sneezing!
10. It is recommended that children under the age of two sit in a rear-facing car seat for extra ___________.

More Practice

Part 1: Read the questions that were seen in the conversation in the beginning of this chapter. How would you answer them in your own words? Write your answers down and practice saying them until it feels natural. (Note: Do not listen to the audio files yet. This will happen in Part 2.)

Example:

***Stella**: My face hurts. Look at it! It's so red, it burns.*

Possible idea ***You***: *Oh! Come here, let me see. This looks like a sunburn. Let's see what we have in the medicine cabinet.*

1. **Stella**: My face hurts. Look at it! It's so red, it burns. (*Chapter 5, Ideas 5-1*)

You:

2. **Doctor**: What have you done to help Liam's asthma attack? (*Chapter 5, Ideas 5-2*)

You:

3. **Pediatrician**: What does Stacy's rash look like? (*Chapter 5, Ideas 5-3*)

You:

4. **Liam**: *Ah-choo!* I don't feel so good. (*Chapter 5, Ideas 5-4*)

You:

5. **Anna**: I can't drink anything! It will make me feel sick! (*Chapter 5, Ideas 5-5*)

You:

Part 2: Go to mindyourlanguage.us/audio-files/ and listen to each question. Pause the audio after the question is asked, and answer it in your own words. Then, restart the audio to hear more ways you could respond to the problems. Repeat these example answers until it feels natural to you.

PRONUNCIATION

Activity 1

Read the words and phrases aloud. Then listen to them at:

mindyourlanguage.us/audio-files/ and repeat.

Chapter 5 > Pronunciation > Activity 1 > Pronunciation 5

out in the sun | I will text your mom
What should I do?
I will give your dad a call | fluid | get better

Activity 2

Listen to the sentences and repeat them aloud. Try practicing the sentences in different ways so that you can use them naturally and confidently in your job.

Go to mindyourlanguage.us/audio-files/

Chapter 1 > Pronunciation > Activity 2

1. Were you out in the sun for a long time today?
2. Put on sunscreen before you go out in the sun.
3. I'm not sure what you should do. I will text your mom right now.
4. She is throwing up. What should I do?
5. Okay, try to drink this glass of water. I will give your dad a call.
6. Lie down on the couch and I will give your mom a call.
7. It is important to drink a lot of fluid so you don't dehydrate.
8. You need fluid. Would you like orange juice, grape juice, or water?
9. You poor thing. You need to get better soon, okay?
10. Why don't you lie down and get some rest so you can feel better?

READING

Notice Board

Read the notices pinned to the bulletin board at a pediatrician's office.

Notice A

Job Opportunity: Babysitter

I am looking for someone to babysit my 8-year-old son, two afternoons per week.

He is allergic to gluten, dairy, nuts, and he has asthma. He uses an inhaler and has an EpiPen. His asthma could be triggered by dust, pollen, and anxiety.

I am seeking someone who has experience working with these types of issues, and who must be trained in First Aid.

Please call me at 555-5555 to discuss pay and schedule an interview. Thank you.

Notice B

Cold or Flu?

It is flu season. Be sure to get vaccinated so you can be protected. What's the difference between a cold and the flu?

With both colds and the flu, the most common symptoms are sore throats, stuffy/runny noses, earaches, sneezing, and coughing.

If you start to experience a serious body ache and a long-lasting fever with the symptoms above, it might be the flu. Do not hesitate to go see a doctor if you think you might have the flu.

Remember to wash your hands, and cover your mouth when you sneeze or cough to avoid spreading germs!

Notice C

JRB Sunscreen

Buy One Get One Free Coupon

Show this coupon to get a free bottle of sunscreen

It must be 100 degrees outside!

When you are going outside this summer, be sure to have protection from the sun:

~stay hydrated!

~wear a hat!

~use an umbrella!

~and most importantly, wear sunscreen!

Coupon available at all participating stores

Notice D

FREE CPR CLASS

Come join our free CPR and Rescue Breathing class on Wednesday, May 19th, at 5:00pm here at Pediatric Associates.

This class will be run by Gregg Orenberg who is a certified CPR and First Aid Trainer.

Space is limited, so RSVP as soon as possible at the front desk.

Activity 1

Choose Notice A, B, C, or D. The first is done as an example.

Which notice is about...

1. A job advertisement? *Notice A*

2. A free class? ___________

3. Ways to avoid getting burnt? ___________

4. A young boy? ___________

5. A comparison between two health issues? ___________

6. Descriptions of symptoms? ___________

7. Learning how to help someone who can't breathe? ___________

8. A coupon? ___________

Activity 2

Answer the following questions based on the Notice Board.

1. Is the health professional job offering a full time position?

A) Yes

B) No

C) Not given

2. What does the advertisement suggest to do if you think you have the flu?

A) Get lots of rest

B) See a doctor

C) Drink fluids

3. When going out in the sun, what is NOT advised in the advertisement?

A) Wear sunscreen

B) Stay hydrated

C) Wear sunglasses

4. How many free sunscreens are available with the coupon?

A) 1

B) 2

C) 3

5. What training is a requirement for the babysitting job?

A) First Aid

B) An online course

C) A PhD

6. Which animals can trigger an asthma attack?

A) Animals with wings

B) Animals with fur

C) Animals who bite

7. When is the CPR class scheduled to take place?

A) May

B) June

C) July

8. What is a runny nose usually a symptom of?

A) A cold

B) The flu

C) An earache

QUESTIONS FOR THOUGHT

Write the answers to the following questions in a journal. Read through your answers at least once a week before you go to work.

1. Out of the five conversations in this chapter, which one did you find the most stressful? Would you have handled it in

the same way or differently? Which conversation was the least stressful? How would you have reacted?

2. Which other types of situations could you use modals and adverbs for speculation? Do you hear this used often? If so, when?
3. Choose one or two new words that you just learned in the vocabulary section of this chapter and use them in conversation this week.
4. Record yourself repeating the sentences in the pronunciation section of this chapter. Listen to it. Do you think you sound confident and clear? What could you work on?
5. Do you often see notices on bulletin boards in doctors' offices? What other types of notices do you usually see? Next time you go into a doctor's office, pay attention to any notices that are pinned to the boards and look at the language points used in them.

GLOSSARY

- **an allergic reaction**

(N) When someone's body responds badly to something they eat, smell, or touch

Example: *After an hour being in a house with cats, my friend's eyes started to water and she began sneezing. We had to leave because of her* ***allergic reaction****.*

- **an antihistamine**

(N) A drug that helps reduce an allergic reaction

Example: *If the swelling doesn't go down in an hour, take an* ***antihistamine****.*

- **anxiety**

(N) A feeling of extreme nervousness or worry

Example: *If he is feeling some* ***anxiety****, try to calm him down.*

- **an asthma attack**

(N) An episode of coughing and shortness of breath

Example: *If you are ever having an* ***asthma attack****, take two puffs of your inhaler and call the doctor.*

- **asthmatic**

(Adj.) Describes a person who has asthma

Example: *She is* ***asthmatic****, so please keep the house clean from dust.*

- **a body ache**

(N) Pain in one's entire body

Example: *I had such a horrible* ***body ache*** *when I had the flu.*

- **dehydrated**

(Adj.) Not having enough fluid in the body

Example: *When he had a stomach virus, we had to take him to the hospital because he was extremely* ***dehydrated****.*

- **discomfort**

(N) Lack of relaxation; physical trouble on the body

Example: *I felt a lot of* ***discomfort*** *when I was sick, so I spent most of my time in bed.*

- **dust**

(N) Dry powder in the air that settles on surfaces

Example: *There was a lot of **dust** in the old classroom, so we spent a lot of time cleaning.*

- **an earache**

(N) Pain in the ear

Example: *She keeps pointing to her ear and saying, "Ouch." I think she has an **earache**.*

- **first aid**

(N) Help for an injured person until doctors can help

Example: *The girl received **first aid** for five minutes until the ambulance arrived to bring her to the hospital.*

- **fluid**

(N) Liquid

Example: *She hasn't been drinking enough **fluid**. Please give her a glass of juice.*

- **food poisoning**

(N) The result of eating spoiled or dangerous food

Example: *I will never go back to that restaurant. I got **food poisoning** the last time I ate there!*

- **hydrated**

(Adj.) Having enough fluid in the body

Example: *I like to drink a glass of water when I first wake up to make me feel* ***hydrated****.*

- **pollen**

(N) Powder that comes from flowers and trees

Example: *The little boy is allergic to* ***pollen****, so let's stay away from those flowers over there.*

- **protection**

(N) Immunity or defense against something dangerous

Example: *The police are here for our* ***protection****.*

- **a rear-facing car seat**

(N) A child's car seat that faces towards the back of the car

Example: *The newborn baby goes in the rear-facing* ***car seat****, and the 3-year-old can face forward.*

- **to snore**

(V) To make a noise while breathing asleep

Example: *The child was* ***snoring*** *so loudly that I needed to wear ear plugs.*

- **a stuffy nose**

(Adj. + N) When one's nose does not allow enough air to breathe

Example: *If you take this antihistamine, it will help with your* ***stuffy nose***.

- **a symptom**

(N) A hint or a sign of something, such as illness

Example: *The doctor knew what was wrong with him because of his* ***symptoms***.

- **to trigger**

(V) To cause the start of an action

Example: *Please don't tease him. He is very tired, so you might* ***trigger*** *a tantrum.*

- **worrisome**

(Adj.) Causing concern

Example: *His behavior was very* ***worrisome***, *so I had a meeting with his teachers and principal.*

CHAPTER 5 ANSWERS

Did You Understand?

1. B
2. A
3. C
4. A
5. A

Language Point: Activity 1

1. D
2. C
3. A
4. B
5. F
6. E
7. H
8. G

Language Point: Activity 2 Possible Answers

1. Abigail + headache + probably + dehydrated

Abigail has a headache. She is probably dehydrated. Let's get her something to drink.

2. Daniel + fever + might + virus

Daniel has a fever. It might be a virus. I am going to call his pediatrician.

3. David + stomach pains + maybe + food poisoning

David has stomach pains. Maybe he has food poisoning from the shrimp he ate at the restaurant. I am going to call his mom.

4. Lilly's ears + red + could + sunburn

Lilly's ears are red. It could be a sunburn. I think I forgot to put sunscreen on her ears.

Vocabulary Activity

1. stuffy nose 2. Hydrated 3. Pollen 4. Triggered 5. body ache 6. anxiety 7. Symptoms 8. first aid 9. Dust 10. protection

Ideas for More Practice

Go to mindyourlanguage.us/audio-files/

Chapter 5 > More Practice

1 Ideas 5-1

Stella: ***My face hurts. Look at it! It's so red, it burns.***

You: Ouch, it looks painful. Did you wear your sunscreen today?

You: Oh, no. Let's put a cold washcloth on it. Were you out in the sun?

You: Oh, poor thing. Let's take care of this sunburn.

2 *Ideas 5-2*

Doctor: ***What have you done to help Liam's asthma attack?***

You: He took 2 puffs of his inhaler.

You: I gave him his inhaler. He took 2 puffs.

You: He's taken his inhaler, 2 puffs of it.

3 *Ideas 5-3*

Pediatrician: ***What does Stacy's rash look like?***

You: Her arms and legs have red bumps all over them.

You: She has itchy red bumps all over her arms and legs.

You: Her arms and legs are covered in bumps about the size of a mosquito bite.

4 *Ideas 5-4*

Liam: ***Ah-choo! I don't feel so good.***

You: Let me get you a tissue. Let's go wash your hands.

You: Oh, no. Let's go rest and drink something warm.

You: Oh, you poor thing. Colds are not fun at all!

5 *Ideas 5-5*

Anna: ***I can't drink anything! It will make me feel sick!***

You: Let's play a game. We can watch TV and every time you hear the word "the," take a small sip. Okay?

You: If you can drink this whole glass in the next 30 minutes, as soon as you're better, I'll take you to the pet store and we can play with all the puppies. How does that sound?

You: I know how you feel. But you know what's worse? If you don't drink it, you will get even sicker, and you might end up needing a needle in your arm. So let's drink slowly together.

Reading

Part 1:

1. A
2. D
3. C
4. A
5. B
6. B
7. D
8. C

Part 2:

1. B
2. B
3. C
4. A
5. A
6. B
7. A
8. A

www.ingramcontent.com/pod-product-compliance
Lightning Source LLC
LaVergne TN
LVHW021345080426
835508LV00020B/2111
* 9 7 8 1 9 3 8 7 5 7 4 1 9 *